I0817331

STONE AGE SCIENCE

ENERGY AND MOVEMENT

Inventions that changed the world—and the science behind them

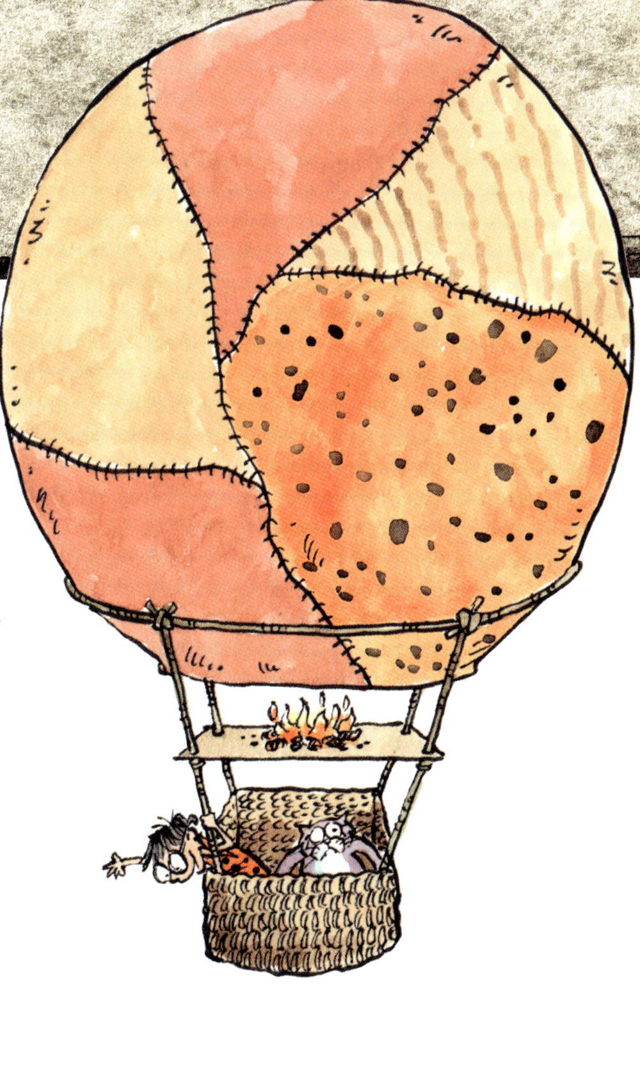

FELICIA LAW & GERRY BAILEY
ILLUSTRATED BY MIKE PHILLIPS

Crabtree Publishing Company
www.crabtreebooks.com
1-800-387-7650

Published in Canada
616 Welland Ave.
St. Catharines, ON
L2M 5V6

Published in the United States
PMB 59051, 350 Fifth Ave.
59th Floor,
New York, NY 10118

Published in **2016 by CRABTREE PUBLISHING COMPANY.**

Authors: Felicia Law and Gerry Bailey
Illustrators: Mike Phillips, Henu Studio
Editors: Shirley Duke, Kelly Spence
Proofreader: Kathy Middleton
Production coordinator and
Prepress technician: Tammy McGarr
Print coordinator: Margaret Amy Salter

Photo credits:
Cover and p1- David M. Schrader
p6 top- Rui Saraiva; middle-
Coqrouge; bottom- ssuaphotos
p9 top- kurt; middle- photosyns
bottom- l i g h t p o e t
p12 top- TongoRo Images Inc; [middle- Action Sports
Photography; bottom- NASA
p16 top- Morrowind; middle -pio3; bottom- Menna
p20 top- Steve Bower; middle- Naihei; bottom- Clearview
stock
p23 top- Danshutter; middle-
Norman Pogson; bottom- Karl R. Martin
p26 top- Zsolt Biczo; middle-
Joe Stone; bottom- revers
p29 top- Siegi; middle- Jay Petersen; bottom- momente

Printed in the USA/082015/SN20150529

Library and Archives Canada Cataloguing in Publication

Law, Felicia, author
Stone Age science : Energy and movement / Felicia Law, Gerry Bailey ; Mike Phillips, illustrator.

(Stone Age science)
Includes index.
Issued in print and electronic formats.
ISBN 978-0-7787-1888-8 (bound).--ISBN 978-0-7787-1913-7 (paperback).--
ISBN 978-1-4271-1677-2 (pdf).--ISBN 978-1-4271-1673-4 (html)

1. Force and energy--Juvenile literature. 2. Dynamics--Juvenile literature. 3. Physics--Juvenile literature. I. Bailey, Gerry, 1945-, author II. Phillips, Mike, 1961-, illustrator III. Title.

QC73.4.L39 2015 j531 C2015-903156-7
C2015-903157-5

Library of Congress Cataloging-in-Publication Data

Law, Felicia, author.
Stone Age science : energy and movement / Felicia Law & Gerry Bailey ; Illustrated by Mike Phillips.
pages cm. -- (Stone Age science)
Includes index.
ISBN 978-0-7787-1888-8 (reinforced library binding : alk. paper) --
ISBN 978-0-7787-1913-7 (pbk. : alk. paper) --
ISBN 978-1-4271-1677-2 (electronic pdf : alk. paper) --
ISBN 978-1-4271-1673-4 (electronic html : alk. paper)
1. Force and energy--Juvenile literature. 2. Dynamics--Juvenile literature. 3. Physics--Juvenile literature. I. Bailey, Gerry, 1945- author. II. Phillips, Mike, 1961- illustrator. III. Title.

QC73.4.L39 2016
531--dc23
2015015335

CONTENTS

MEET LEO

Meet Leo, the brightest kid on the block.

Bright as in IQ off the scale, inventive as in Leonardo da Vinci inventive, and way, way ahead of his time...

So that's Leo!

Block as in Stone Age block. Stone Age as in 30,000 years ago.

Then there's Pallas—Leo's pet.

Pallas is wild. His ancestors have been around for millions of years. You won't see many Pallas cats around today, unless you happen to be visiting the icy, cold wasteland of Arctic Siberia in northern Russia.

And there's a cast of other characters who are all inventors—sort of!

THE KITE

"Great!" says Leo. "We've been invited to the chief's party tonight. He wants everyone to come."

"We?" repeats Pallas. "Am I invited, too?"

"Actually, he didn't mention you," says Leo. "But he does mention everyone else. How am I going to let them know?"

"Well, don't ask me to help," grumbles Pallas. "It's YOUR invitation."

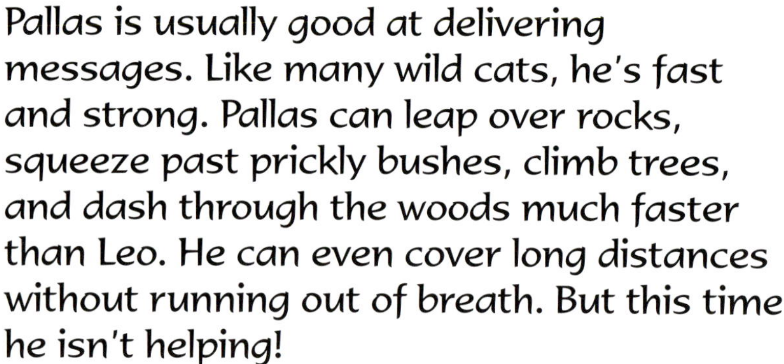

Pallas is usually good at delivering messages. Like many wild cats, he's fast and strong. Pallas can leap over rocks, squeeze past prickly bushes, climb trees, and dash through the woods much faster than Leo. He can even cover long distances without running out of breath. But this time he isn't helping!

"I just need to get those invitations delivered," sighs Leo. "Can't you think of any good ideas, Pallas? I promise you can come, too—if you help me with this."

"Airmail is fast," says Pallas. "The invitations could be sent by air."

- *Leo could tape the invitation to the leg of a bird—then hope it flies in the right direction.*
- *Or, he could spear the invitations to the tip of an arrow and shoot them in the direction they need to go.*

A kite is a kind of aircraft. It is made of material, such as cloth or paper, that is stretched over a frame. A kite uses the **force** of the wind to fly. It is guided by a long string from the kite to the ground. A tail gives a kite **stability** to keep it upright.

The first kites were invented by the Chinese around 1000 BCE. These kites were used by the army for different tasks, such as sending messages. Today, flying kites is a fun hobby. Kites are also used by scientists to carry tools such as thermometers into the **atmosphere** to study the weather.

There are four forces of flight that help a kite soar through the air. Wind pressure pushes on the kite from below creating an upward force known as **lift**. **Weight** is the force of gravity pressing downward on the kite. Created by the stretching of the line, **thrust** is the force that moves the kite forward. **Drag** is a backward pull on the kite created by **air resistance**.

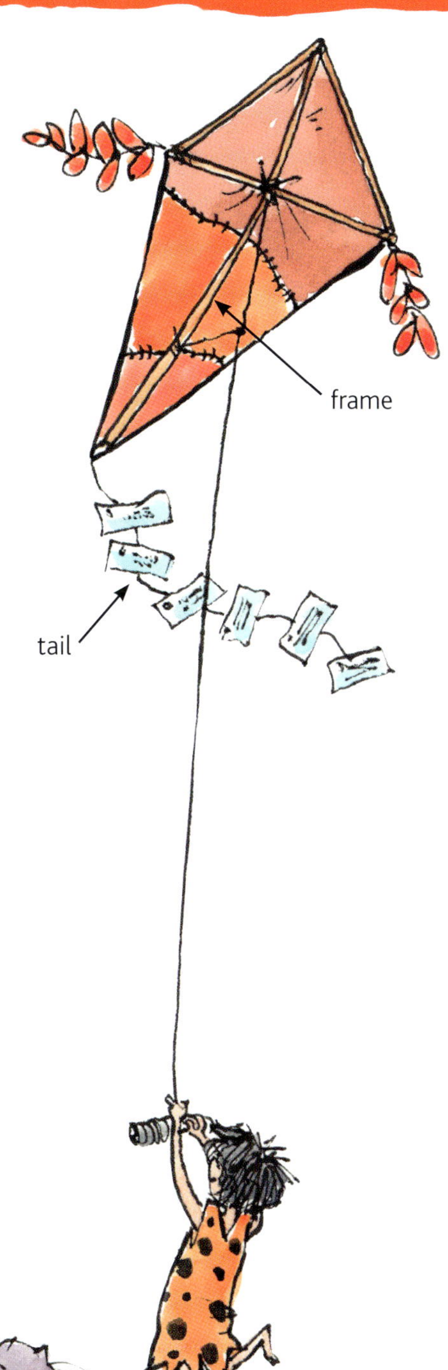

WIND ENERGY

Wind **energy** describes how the movement of the wind is used to make something move. This movement is often used to power machines. For example, in a windmill, energy from the wind pushes against the **sails**, or blades, which then turn a wheel inside. Sailboats also use wind energy to push against the sails and move the boat forward.

Moving things, such as wind or water, have energy that can be used to power something else. This kind of energy is called **kinetic energy**. Kinetic comes from the Greek word for "move." All moving things have kinetic energy.

Even things that are not moving have a kind of energy. For example, an apple in a tree may not be moving, but it could move. When it is ripe, it will drop to the ground. The energy it stores in its hanging position is called **potential energy**. As the apple falls, its potential energy will turn into kinetic energy.

Windmills are often used to grind corn and flour, and to generate electricity.

Sails on a boat can be moved to catch as much wind as possible.

Sand yachts race along the beach on wheels with the help of the wind.

MAKE A KITE

You will need

- *Two lightweight wooden sticks: one 16 inches (40 cm) long and one 24 inches (60 cm) long*
- *string*
- *scissors*
- *colorful wrapping paper*
- *glue*
- *paper clips*
- *tape*

1. *Tie the center of the short stick across the longer one about 8 inches (20 cm) from the top to form a cross. Next, knot the string to each point to form a diamond-shaped frame.*

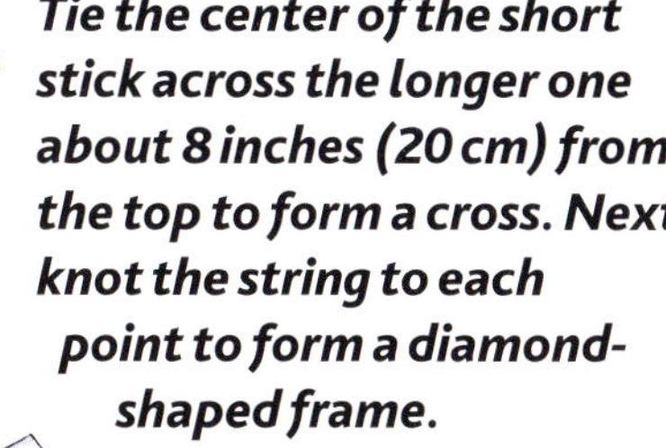

2. *Lay the frame on a sheet of wrapping paper and trace around it leaving a one-inch (2.5 cm) border. Cut the paper out and attach it to the frame by folding the paper over and gluing it.*

3. *Measure halfway between the center of the cross and the short ends. Carefully tie one piece of string about 16 inches (40 cm) long to each side.*

4. *Tie the string that will be your line to a paper clip or wire loop, then hook the paperclip onto the kite's loop of string. This makes a harness for your line to help the kite fly more easily.*

5. *Make a tail for your kite by knotting paper bows at equal distances along a long piece of string. Attach it to the bottom corner of the kite.*

THE LONGBOW

Leo wants to scare away an eagle that is circling in the sky.
"I don't want it to dive at you, Pallas, while it's looking for its dinner!"

A **longbow** was a bow used by **archers** in the **Middle Ages**. A longbow was as tall as an archer, and the arrows fired from it were half the height. In the 1300s, armies could fire from far away in battle because longbows could send an arrow over a great distance. Archers could shoot up to 20 arrows a minute from a distance of about 900 feet (275 m) away.

The longbow was usually made of wood from the yew tree because it is flexible. Elm wood could also be used. It is believed to have taken about 100 pounds (45 kg) of pressure to pull the great bow, so archers needed to have strong back and arm muscles.

PALLAS SUGGESTS...

- *Leo could send a mosquito up to bite the eagle. Mosquito bites are very itchy!*
- *Or, Leo could use his darts and throw them as high as he could—but would they reach high enough?*

ELASTICITY

Elasticity describes how well a material can spring back to its original shape when it has been bent or stretched. An **elastic**, or flexible, material can bend without breaking. For example, paper and plastic, are very elastic materials. An iron rod is not.

Materials are sometimes measured by their **elastic limit**. This is the maximum amount they can stretch and still return to their original shape. If the stretch goes beyond this limit, the material will become permanently bent. Materials bend because of **stress**, or the force put on them. How much a material bends or changes shape is measured as **strain**.

If the strain on a longbow is too high, it can't be bent. If the strain is too low, the longbow will bend too much and it will have too little power to shoot the arrow very far.

Longbows were used in battle until the invention of firearms.

A traditional longbow and arrow

The flexibility of the bow helps the arrow fly away at a high speed.

THE PARACHUTE

Pallas climbed up the tree, but he has no idea how to get down! This is not unusual.

Leo suggests to Pallas that he should just close his eyes and jump. They'll all be there to catch him—well, they'll try!

The trouble is that Pallas is round and solid, so he will fall very fast if he jumps. Unless there is some way of slowing him down...

PALLAS SUGGESTS...

- *Why can't I just spread my arms and then the air would hold me up—just like it does for a bird?* 
- *Or, maybe I could float down holding onto a large balloon. I just need to find a balloon—or something else I can fill with air.*

A **parachute** is a device used to slowly lower people or objects through the air and allow them to land safely. The part of the parachute that opens to catch the air is called the **canopy**. The canopy is usually rectangular, or shaped like an umbrella.

Parachutes are made from lightweight fabric. The first parachutes were made from silk. Since the 1940s, most parachutes have been made of **nylon**, a tough, light fabric. Cords called suspension lines attach the canopy to a harness that holds the person or object. When the parachute is closed, it folds into a small pack. To release the parachute, the user pulls a handle called a ripcord.

Parachutes were first used to descend from gas-filled balloons in the late 18th century. Today they are used for jumping out of planes, landing soldiers in battle, and skydiving.

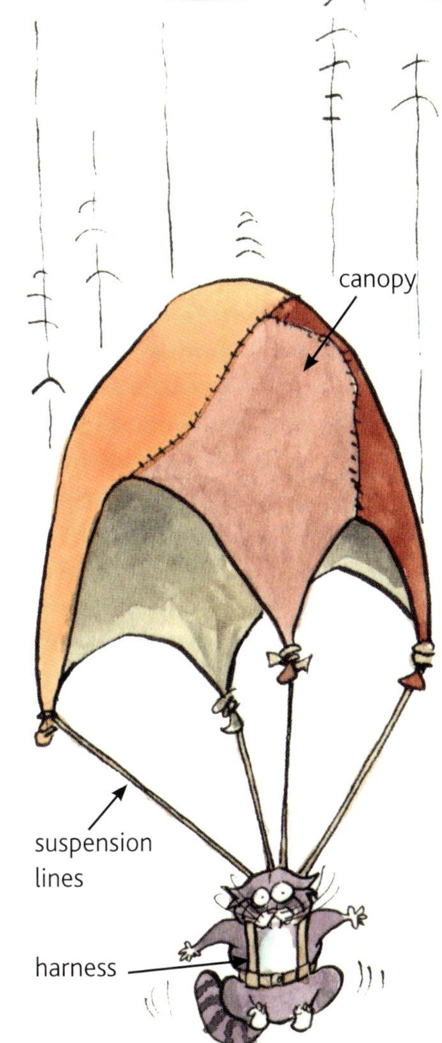

AIR RESISTANCE

When an object moves through the air, the air pushes against the object, slowing down the movement. This is called air resistance. The object that is moving rubs against the gases that make up the air. Air resistance slows down a parachute so that people falling through the air can drift slowly and safely to the ground below.

Modern parachutes use air resistance to glide slowly down through the air.

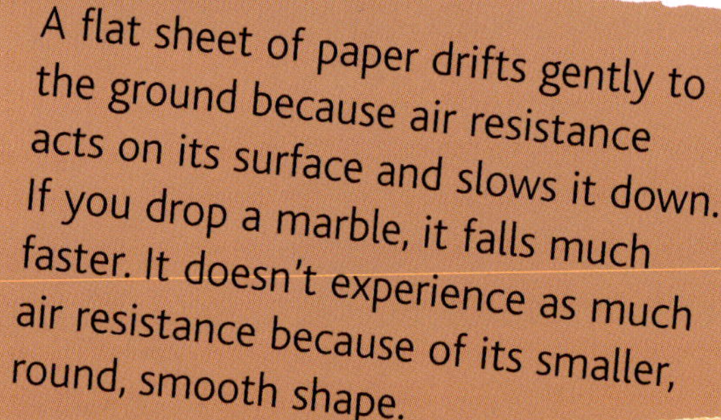

A flat sheet of paper drifts gently to the ground because air resistance acts on its surface and slows it down. If you drop a marble, it falls much faster. It doesn't experience as much air resistance because of its smaller, round, smooth shape.

A drag racing car has no brakes, so it must stop with the help of a parachute.

Early airplanes used air resistance to slow down as they landed. The landing gear and other parts that stuck out from the plane's body rubbed against the air. Today, modern planes have a body shape that is **streamlined**, or smoother, and can move through the air with much less resistance.

Parachutes bring astronauts safely back to Earth in their space capsule.

MAKE A PAPER PARACHUTE

You will need

- *two pieces of tissue paper*
- *glue* • *string*
- *tape*
- *cardboard*
- *a pencil* • *paint*
- *scissors* • *a paintbrush*

1. *Cut out two large squares of tissue paper. Glue the pieces together.*

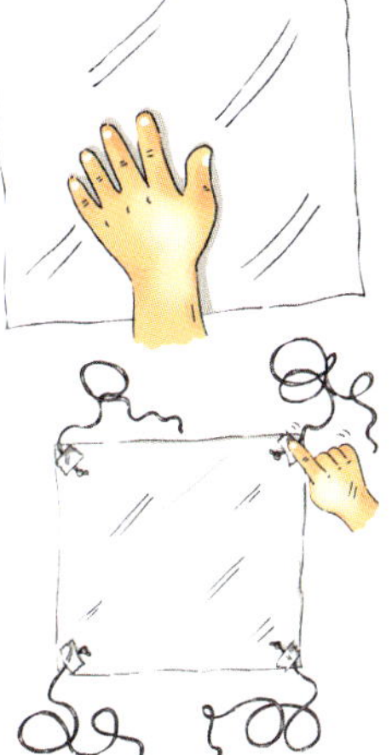

2. *Attach equal lengths of string to each corner of the parachute with some tape.*

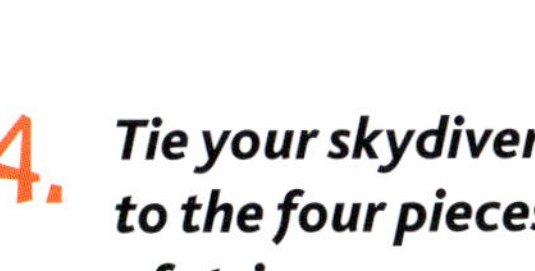

3. *Draw a skydiver on a piece of cardboard. Cut it out and paint it.*

4. *Tie your skydiver to the four pieces of string.*

5. *Take your parachute outside and drop it from a high place to see it float gently to the ground.*

THE WINDMILL

Leo has been busy gathering the wild grain that grows along the riverbank. There is still a lot to harvest. When it's cut, he'll separate the grains from the husks and pound them into flour.

Pallas isn't interested in cutting wheat or pounding grain. But he does enjoy crunchy bread and tasty cookies that are made from the flour.

"Help me, Pallas," says Leo. "Help me crush the grains of wheat into flour. Then I promise I'll bake us both a delicious harvest cake."

Pallas complains, but he actually starts to enjoy hammering the grains into powder—for a while! But soon, his arm starts to ache.

Leo looks at the tiny pile of flour that Pallas has ground. "OK," he says. "There must be a better way."

PALLAS SUGGESTS...

- *Leo could pound the grain with a mortar and pestle—a kind of bowl and club. But this would require muscle power, too.*
- *Or, Leo could grind the grain with a huge* ***roller****—or two huge rollers. Maybe he could think of some way to power these heavy rollers.*

A windmill is a machine that uses the power of wind. Its **blades**, called sails, are pushed by the wind. When wind pushes the sails, it causes them to turn. This movement creates kinetic energy.

The early settlers in North America often used wind power. Grain was ground into flour at gristmills, which were usually powered by water or wind. Wind turned the sails, which turned a grinding stone.

A fantail is a smaller sail wheel that is attached to the back of the mill. It is fastened to a gear that moves the grinding room of the gristmill around to face the wind.

USING WIND POWER

Wind power describes the use of the wind to operate machines, generate electricity, or turn a propeller. To operate a machine, wind energy is used to push an object. The object may be as simple as the **sail** of a boat. The wind pushes against the sail to make the boat move across the water.

You use your very own wind energy—a puff of air—to spin a pinwheel.

A modern wind **generator**, also called a **turbine**, is a machine that produces electricity. It works in the same way. On top, it has a propeller that is similar to what you see on some airplanes. When the wind pushes against the propeller, it turns very quickly. The propeller then turns a generator that makes electricity.

It takes many wind generators, or turbines, to produce enough electricity for a small town.

A **wind pump** is a special kind of propeller with many blades that is often used to drain wet areas to become farmland. A windpump has a fantail at the back. The fantail always pushes the wind pump to face the direction from which the wind is coming. The propeller powers a machine that pumps water out of the ground.

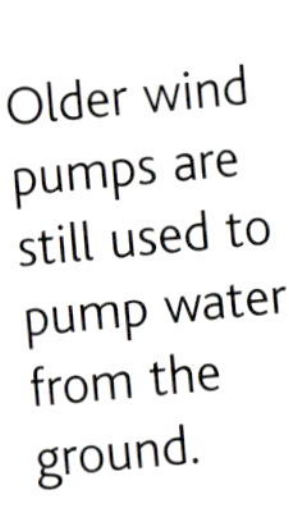

Older wind pumps are still used to pump water from the ground.

MAKE A WIND TURBINE

You will need

- a 1-quart (1 liter) drink carton
- sand, gravel, or dirt
- glue • a pin • a pencil
- a drinking straw
- a bottle cork
- a thin bamboo skewer
- a soft drink bottle cap
- thick card • paint

1. To keep your model from falling over, fill the carton with sand, gravel, or dirt, then glue the opening closed again.

2. Make a hole with a pin on opposite sides of the carton. Enlarge the holes with a pencil and push a drinking straw through them. Trim the straw, leaving about two inches (5 cm) on each side. Add a roof if you like.

3. Make a hole through the center of a cork and push the stick through it. Then make the turbine by gluing squares of index cards around the cork. Let it dry completely.

4. Attach the turbine to one end of the straw. At the other end, attach a reel made from a bottle top and cardboard. Paint and decorate your finished model.

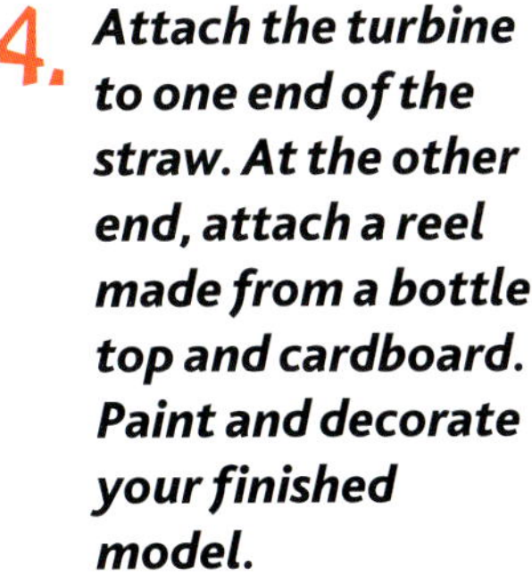

5. Place your wind turbine at the edge of a table and tie an object to a string attached to the reel. Blow hard to raise the load.

Try experimenting with different-sized objects!

THE HOT AIR BALLOON

Leo is going on a trip
"Where are you going?" asks Pallas.
"WE," says Leo. "Where are WE going? And the answer is, we're going for a ride in the sky."

Pallas wants to know how. Well, he doesn't really want to know because he guesses it will involve doing something dangerous—like flying, or jumping from a great height. And Pallas doesn't like heights—or flying and jumping, for that matter.

Leo says he wants to build a machine that will float over the countryside and carry them high above the ground. He has built a huge balloon and filled it with air. But it won't rise at all! Leo doesn't know what to do.

PALLAS SUGGESTS...

- *Pallas says that Leo's laundry is very heavy when it's wet. But, as soon as it's dried by the Sun, it's light enough to flap in the warm air.*
- *Don't birds spread their wings and soar on the warm air that rises off the ground? Maybe Leo could use warm air!*

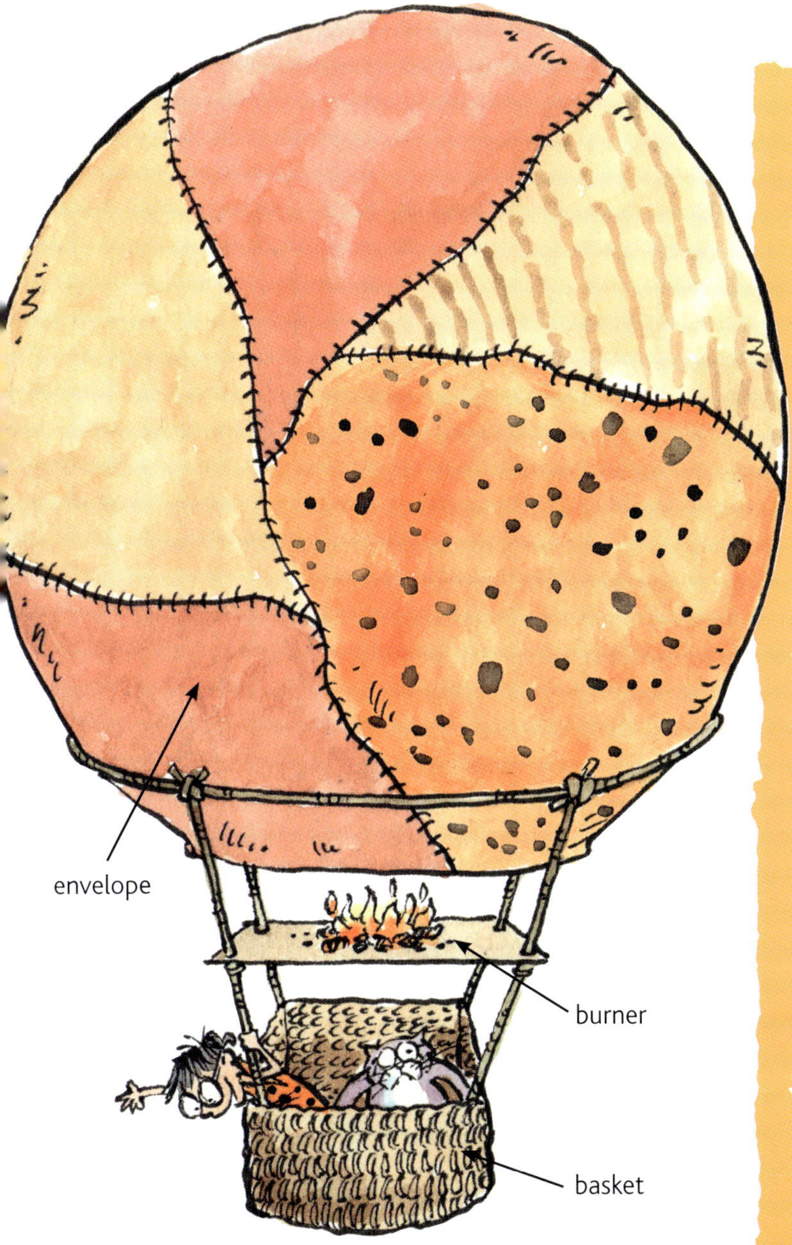

envelope

burner

basket

Hot air has less **density** than cooler air. A hot air balloon is a flying machine powered by hot air. The balloon is made from a large bag called an envelope. The first balloons were round, but today balloons are made in almost every shape.

The envelope is attached by ropes to a basket where the passengers ride. Most balloons are filled with hot air, generated from a **burner** located under the balloon. Most burners use a gas called propane. Lightweight gases such as helium or hydrogen can also be used to power a balloon.

Gas-powered balloons are also used by scientists to carry instruments high into the atmosphere to record and collect data about weather.

MOVING MOLECULES

All simple substances are made up of tiny pieces of material called **atoms**. A **molecule** is a group of two or more atoms that are bonded together. For example, a molecule of water contains two atoms of hydrogen and one atom of the gas oxygen. Molecules are so tiny that one drop of water contains millions of them.

Today, most balloons are made of nylon.

When molecules are cold, they stay close together and do not move very much. However, when molecules are heated they gain energy and speed up. They bounce off of each other, spreading apart. Molecules in hot air move around faster than molecules in cold air.

Hot air lanterns are released into the sky during festivals.

Faster-moving molecules in hot air take up more space than slower moving molecules in cold air, so there are fewer of them in the same amount of space. With fewer molecules, the hot air in the space is lighter, so it rises. A hot air balloon uses moving molecules to make it rise.

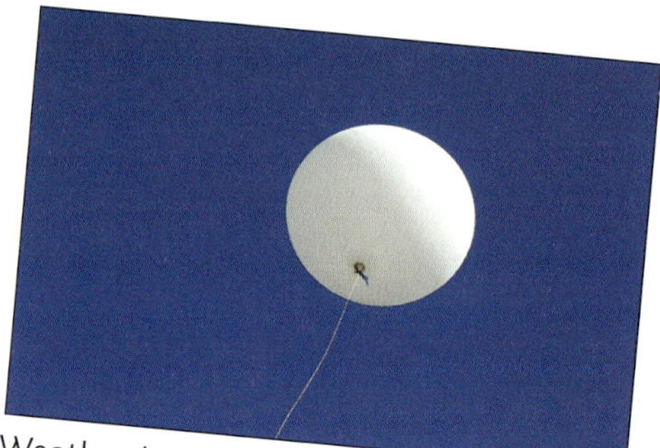

Weather balloons are sent high into the sky to collect and send back information about the weather.

MAKE A BALLOON MOBILE

You will need

- *a balloon*
- *string*
- *newspaper*
- *a paste made of one cup (236 ml) of flour and two cups (473 ml) of water*
- *paint*
- *colored paper*
- *a small box*
- *fabric*
- *tape*
- *8 thumbtacks*
- *plastic spoons*

1. ***Hang a balloon from a string. Cover it with layers of newspaper scraps soaked in the paste mixture. Let each layer dry before the next layer is put on.***

2. ***Paint and decorate the balloon.***

3. ***Cover a small box in fabric or colored paper.***

4. ***Cut eight pieces of string into equal lengths and tie a knot at one end of each. Attach the knotted ends to the inside of the balloon basket with tape.***

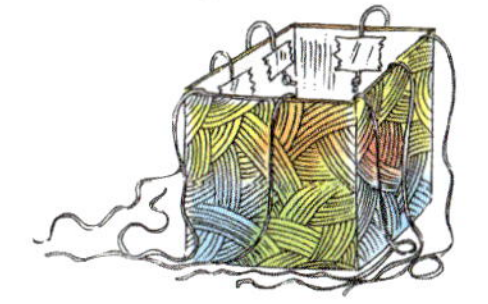

5. ***Stick eight thumbtacks around the base of the balloon. Wind the other end of the pieces of string around the thumbtacks and glue. Make passengers by painting faces onto plastic spoons.***

THE SPEAR

Leo uses a sharpened flint stone to cut things. Flint is one of the hardest kinds of rock so it cuts easily. However, Leo can't hunt animals with a flint. He'd have to get much too close to the animals—and many of them are dangerous.

The other hunters use spears to hunt large cats, wild boar, reindeer, bison, and elk. They are very skilled hunters. In fact, spear throwing is a skill a hunter has to master at a young age.

Leo ties his flint to a long pole. Now he has a spear, but he still needs a lot of practice. "If you stand very still," he tells Pallas, "I can practice throwing the spear past your head. Okay?"

"Not okay!" cries Pallas.

PALLAS SUGGESTS...

- *Pallas suggests Leo start by practicing with a dart made from soft tree bark.*
- *But, if Leo wants something that moves faster and farther, he must use a spear. The point of a spear cuts through the air just like the pointed front of a canoe cuts through water.*

AERODYNAMICS

When an object moves through air, the air rubs against it. This rubbing, called **friction**, slows the object down. Scientists and engineers try to design objects so they will create as little friction as possible. An object that reduces friction in this way is said to be **aerodynamic**, or streamlined.

A racing shell is a long, slim boat used in rowing. It cuts easily through the water.

In prehistoric times, people made spears and arrowheads from sharpened flint stones. The flint head was bound with cord to a long wooden pole, or **shaft.** The spear could be thrown a great distance because of its aerodynamic shape.

Modern, high-speed trains have bullet-shaped noses to help them reduce friction and travel quickly.

Aerodynamics is the study of the forces that act on an object as it moves through the air. It is an important feature when designing and building moving things such as airplanes, rockets, and cars. An airplane is very aerodynamic. Its sharp, streamlined nose allows it to easily fly through the air.

Fighter planes are aerodynamic, which helps them to fly at great speeds.

THE BATTERY

Leo can't see in the dark. He stumbles and trips and has no idea where he is going. But Pallas, being a cat, CAN see in the dark. "Follow me!" he says.

But Leo can't even see Pallas!

"If only the moon were shining," says Leo. But it isn't.

Cave Bear lives in the dark and he can see where he's going, too. "You humans should stay home at night," he says. "Maybe one day you'll learn how to light things up. You aren't the fastest learners!"

CAVE BEAR SUGGESTS

- *Cave Bear suggests Leo use Saber Tooth as a guide. She has bright eyes that shine in the dark. Her eyes are even larger than Pallas's eyes.*
- *Cave Bear also suggests that Leo gather some shining glowworms in a tube to make a glowworm flashlight.*

A **battery** is a metal container that stores a chemical mixture. Batteries turn **chemical energy** into **electrical energy**. Batteries provide electricity where there are no electrical outlets available for plugging in devices.

When a device that contains batteries is turned on, the metals and chemicals inside the batteries react to each other.

This **chemical reaction** creates an electric current that flows out of the batteries, powering the devices containing them.

Some batteries are **disposable**. This means that when one of the chemicals inside run outs, the battery cannot be used again. Other batteries are **rechargeable**, which means they can be refilled with electricity and used again.

CHEMICAL ENERGY

The whole universe is made up of chemicals. These are mixed together in different ways. As they mix, and sometimes heat up, they change. This creates chemical energy.

Burning wood and coal releases chemical energy that helps light and heat our lives.

Chemical energy helps make things move. The chemical energy released by the food you eat helps you move. The chemical energy released by burning fuels, such as wood or coal, produces heat energy. Burning fuels also helps power fast-moving vehicles and machines.

Fireworks contain chemical explosives. When the explosive is lit, it creates bright sparks that are thrown in all directions.

Electricity is a type of energy. In a battery, electricity is made by converting chemical energy into electrical energy. The electrical energy we use in our homes is made in a factory called a power plant. Both kinetic and chemical energy are changed into electrical energy at power plants.

A battery stores chemical energy which is turned into electrical energy to power a flashlight.

MAKE A BATTERY MOTOR

You will need

- *copper wire*
- *two C-batteries*
- *a hammer and nails* • *tape*
- *a rectangular piece of board*
- *a plastic cup* • *strong glue*
- *an empty paper roll*
- *five circular magnets*

1. ***Coil a long strip of wire around in a loop five times and leave the ends sticking out, as shown:***

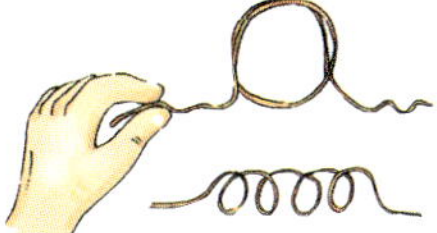

2. ***Ask an adult to help you hammer nails into a board on each side of the two C-batteries. Make sure the batteries are tightly connected, then hammer a nail at each end to hold them in place.***

3. ***Glue a cup to the top of the paper roll. Put two magnets on top of the cup and three inside the bottom of the cup. Glue the paper roll to the board.***

4. ***Force a piece of wire between the nail and the top end of the front battery. Run it along the board and up the cup tower, taping it to the outside. Leave a length of wire sticking up above the cup***

5. ***Repeat the entire process for the back nail. Make a small loop in the wires above the cup.***

6. ***Set each end of the copper coil into one of the loops above the cup tower, making sure the bottom of the coil is above the magnets leaving a space about as thick as a paper clip. The coil should begin to spin.***

MICHAEL FARADAY

A MAMMOTH INVENTOR!

Michael Faraday was born in 1791 and died in 1867.

Michael grew up in a small village near London, England. His father was a poor blacksmith, and his family did not always have a lot of food to eat. Although he didn't go to school, Michael learned to read and write.

He became interested in science from reading books. He began experimenting with electricity and made a simple battery. His enthusiasm led to a job with Sir Humphrey Davy, a famous chemist at the Royal Institution in London.

Soon, Michael became a respected scientist himself. He studied chemistry and physics. After much study, he believed he could create an electric current in a wire using magnets because they both involved forces.

After many experiments, Michael was able to produce a continuous current by spinning a wire-wrapped copper disk between the poles of a magnet. This invention was the first generator.

A generator is a device that changes **mechanical energy** into electrical energy. Mechanical energy is created by the movement of an object. Inside a simple generator, a coil of wire rotates within a **magnetic field**, which is a space affected by magnets.

Electrical generators in modern cars are called alternators.

As the coil turns, the movement creates a flow of electric current in the wire. As the coil rotates faster, it generates more electricity. The energy produced by a generator is measured in units called volts. Today, generators can be powered by many sources, including wind, water, steam, and gas, to power different machines, such as a car engine.

This huge generator supplies a whole factory with electrical power.

Faraday's groundbreaking discovery changed the way people looked at electricity and how it could be created.

Inside a generator, coils of wire quickly spin inside a magnetic field.

WARM AIR EXPANDS

See for yourself what happens when you warm up air and water.

You will need:
modeling clay, an empty bottle, a drinking straw, a bowl, a cloth

1. Seal a straw into the neck of a bottle using modeling clay.

2. Hold the bottle upside down and dip the end of the straw into a bowl of warm water.

3. Wrap the bottle with a warm wet cloth to heat the air inside. When you see bubbles in the water, that means the air in the bottle has expanded and is escaping.

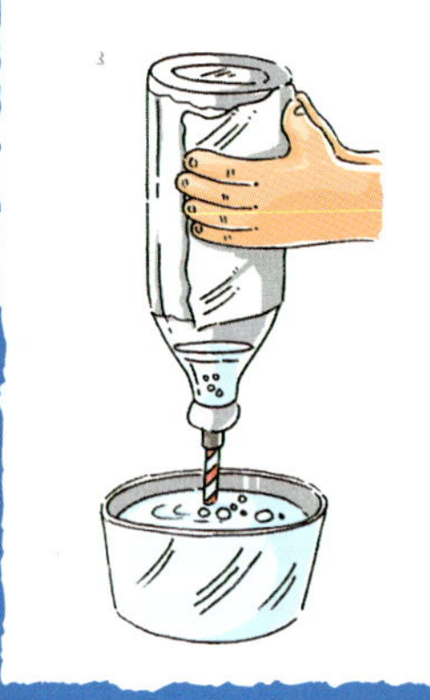

4. Next, replace the warm cloth with a cold one. This makes the air in the bottle shrink so it takes up less space. The water will now rise up into the bottle because there is less air to push it out.

5. Finally, fill the bottle with cold water. Put the straw back, holding it in with clay. Some water will rise up the straw. Now place the bottle in a bowl of hot water. You will see the water rise even farther up the straw. Heat has made the water expand.

GLOSSARY

Note: Some boldfaced words are defined where they appear in the book.

aerodynamic Describes how easily an object moves through the air

air resistance The way air pushes against an object, slowing it down as it moves

archer A person who shoots with a bow and arrow

atmosphere The gases that surround Earth

atom A tiny part of the material that makes up the universe

battery A metal container with a chemical mixture that can be made to produce electricity to power machines

burner A fuel-burning or heat-producing device where a flame or heat is made

chemical energy Energy that's stored in the bonds of molecules. It changes to other forms of energy such as heat or light when it is broken down .

chemical reaction The breaking or making of chemical bonds

density Describing how compact or tightly packed something is

electric current The flow of postive or negative particles, such as electrons

electrical energy The energy produced by an electrical current

energy Power generated from physical or chemical reactions, often used to provide light and heat, and operate machines

force Another name for a push or a pull. Forces do work and make things move or change their shape.

friction The dragging force that slows objects down when they rub or move against each other

kinetic energy The energy that objects have when they are moving.

magnet A piece of material that attracts certain metals

Middle Ages The period in Europe from about 500 BCE to 1500 BCE

power plants Buildings in which electricity for a large area is generated

rechargeable Able to be refilled with energy

rollers Large cylinderswhich are used to move, press, shape, spread, or smooth something

stability The quality of not easily being moved or changed

turbine An engine driven by a shaft fitted with a number of blades; The blades turn when pushed by air, steam, or water.

LEARNING MORE

Books

Experiments in Forces and Motion with Toys and Everyday Stuff by Emily Sohn. Capstone, 2015

Force and Motion by Lewis Parker. Perfection Learning, 2014

Forces and Motion by Leon Gray. Gareth Stevens Publishing, 2013

Websites

Explore more science activities and experiments.
www.education.com/activity/physical-science/

Experiments, fun facts, and interactive games help give readers a better understanding of scientific concepts.
www.sciencekids.co.nz/physics.html

Read about pioneers in the development of electricity.
www.enwin.com/kids/electricity/energy_pioneers.cfm

INDEX